EASY TAPAS

EASY TAPAS

Spanish Snacks to Serve with Drinks

JULZ BERESFORD

PHOTOGRAPHY BY PETER CASSIDY

RYLAND
PETERS
& SMALL

LONDON NEW YORK

Senior Designer	Paul Tilby
Commissioning Editor	Elsa Petersen-Schepelern
Editor	Susan Stuck
Production	Patricia Harrington
Art Director	Gabriella Le Grazie
Publishing Director	Alison Starling
Food Stylist	Linda Tubby
Props Stylist	Róisín Nield
Editorial Consultant	Luis Peral Aranda

First published in the USA in 2004
10 9 8 7 6 5 4 3 2

by Ryland Peters & Small, Inc.
519 Broadway, 5th Floor, New York, NY 10012

Text © Julz Beresford 2004
Design and photographs © Ryland Peters & Small 2004

Printed and bound in China

Library of Congress Cataloging-in-Publication Data

Beresford, Julz.

  Easy tapas : Spanish snacks to serve with cocktails / Julz
Beresford ; photography by Peter Cassidy.

    p. cm.

Includes bibliographical references and index.

  ISBN 1-84172-580-3

1. Appetizers. 2. Snack foods. 3. Cookery, Spanish. I. Title.

TX740.B465 2003

641.8'12--dc22

                          2003017031

NOTES

All spoon measurements are level unless otherwise stated.

Grills, ovens, and broilers should be heated to the required
temperature before adding the food.

Specialist Spanish ingredients are available in larger
supermarkets, Spanish and sometimes Italian delicatessens,
and also by mail order.

The author recommends:
www.tienda.com,
3701 Rochambeau Road, Williamsburg VA 23188

Stavis Seafoods
www.stavis.com
Suite 305, Fish Pier West,
212 Northern Avenue, Boston MA 02210

ACKNOWLEDGMENTS

I would like to thank the team who made this book so beautiful. I know that individually they put one hundred
percent effort into all they do. Thanks especially to Elsa for all her hard work and patience, and to Luis, who
helped so much with the book. I'd like to thank my Mum, Dad, Nan, and Kate with a special thank you to my
brother Tim—you are an inspiration and without your constant support and encouragement I never would
have achieved what I have. Richard, thank you for being you and letting me be just me.

contents

TAPAS

Wherever you are in Spain, you're never far away from a friendly tapas bar. Sit, eat, drink, and share in the friendly topical conversations. Sit, wonder, and admire the splendors of these pre-dinner dishes.

The origins of tapas have long been debated. Thought to originate in Andalusia, some claim it originated as a lid or covering—a *tapa* for your wine to stop insects getting in. Others say it was served by the innkeepers as an accompaniment to wine to help keep the coach drivers sober. However, an early version was certainly just a slice of ham, and as all bartenders will tell you, salty foods make people want to drink more. Whatever the reason, tapas have been around as long as anyone can remember.

In this book I have collected authentic recipes, representative of many regions in Spain. The south varies considerably from the north, as does the coast to the inland. Each place and every bar has its own version of tapas.

The use of cured meat and salted fish is common all over Spain and these are now widely available around the world. So experiment and bring those flavors of Spain to your own table.

Through my travels and love of all things Spanish I have written from the heart. I hope by cooking my recipes you will discover how easy it is to prepare tapas and relish how delicious these little dishes can be.

And remember, the key to great tapas is always good food, good wine, and good conversation.

GAZPACHO

Gazpacho is a light summer soup. It originated in the south of Spain, traditionally in Andalusia. For best results use ripe tomatoes and a good-quality olive oil—but, most importantly, serve it icy cold.

Grind the garlic and salt together using a mortar and pestle.

Put the bread in a saucer with a little water and let soak. Put the garlic, bread, tomatoes, onion, cucumber, and vinegar in a blender and purée until smooth. Keeping the machine running, add the oil in a slow and steady stream. Add salt and pepper to taste, then add the sugar.

Pour the mixture through a strainer into a bowl, adding more salt, pepper, and vinegar if necessary. Chill in the refrigerator overnight and serve in small bowls or glasses with a little chopped cucumber on top.

1 garlic clove

a pinch of coarse salt

1 slice white bread, crusts removed

4 ripe juicy tomatoes, peeled and seeded

1 tablespoon grated onion

¼ small cucumber, peeled and seeded, plus extra to serve

1 tablespoon Spanish red wine vinegar

2 tablespoons olive oil

1 teaspoon sugar

freshly ground black pepper

SERVES 4

TORTILLA ESPAÑOLA
SPANISH OMELET

1 cup olive oil

4 potatoes, about 1 lb.,
cut into ½-inch cubes

1 onion, thinly sliced

6 eggs

coarse salt and freshly
ground black pepper

*a deep skillet, 9 inches
diameter*

SERVES 4

Tortilla española is recognized as Spain's national dish. It's a favorite, eaten at all times of the day. Everywhere I've been, tapas bars have had this delicious tortilla ready to be cut and served. It can be made in advance and it even tastes better that way.

Heat the oil in a skillet until hot, add the potatoes and onion, turn to coat with the oil, then reduce the temperature. Cook for about 15 minutes or until soft, turning often without letting them brown. Remove the potatoes and onions with a slotted spoon and drain on paper towels. Pour the oil into a small bowl.

Put the eggs, salt, and pepper in a bowl and beat with a fork. Add the potatoes and onions to the bowl, stir gently, then set aside for 10 minutes.

Put 2 tablespoons of the reserved oil in the skillet and heat until smoking. Pour in the potato and egg mixture, spreading the potatoes evenly in the pan. Cook for 1 minute, then reduce the heat to medium and shake the skillet often to stop it sticking. When the eggs are brown underneath and the top nearly firm, put a plate the same size as the skillet on the top and flip the omelet onto the plate. Add ¼ cup of the remaining oil to the skillet and slide the omelet back into the skillet to brown the other side. Lower the heat to low and flip the omelet 3 more times, cooking 1 minute each side, to help give it a good shape while cooking. It should remain juicy inside.

Transfer to a plate, brush the top with oil, and let stand until cool. Serve in squares or wedges.

CHAMPIÑONES RELLENOS
STUFFED MUSHROOMS

8 medium mushrooms

2 tablespoons milk

2 tablespoons
bread crumbs

2 tablespoons finely
chopped onion

1 garlic clove, crushed

1 tablespoon
freshly chopped
flat-leaf parsley

2 tablespoons
ground pork

1 tablespoon finely
chopped jamón serrano
(Spanish ham),
prosciutto, or Smithfield

olive oil

1 tablespoon canned
chopped pimiento

1 tablespoon freshly
squeezed lemon juice

SERVES 4

Almost every town or region has its own version of this dish. I found this one on the east coast of Spain, and often saw variations of it in Catalonia. I think what makes it so special is the unique taste of Spanish ham, which is now becoming more widely available in other parts of the world.

Clean the mushrooms and remove the stems. Finely chop 2 of the stems and put them in a bowl. Add the milk and bread crumbs and let soak for 10 minutes.

Add the onion, garlic, parsley, ground pork, and ham. Mix well, cover with plastic wrap and let marinate in the refrigerator overnight.

When ready to cook, put 1 heaping teaspoon of the mixture in each of the mushroom caps. Swirl over a little olive oil, then cook in a preheated oven at 350°F for 15 minutes.

Remove from the oven, add a little chopped pimiento to each one, and sprinkle with lemon juice. Serve warm.

BOQUERONES EN VINAGRE
MARINATED ANCHOVIES

6 oz. fresh anchovies*

scant ½ cup good-quality white vinegar

3 garlic cloves, sliced

1 tablespoon chopped fresh flat-leaf parsley

scant ½ cup olive oil

SERVES 4

If fresh anchovies are unavailable, use any small fish, such as smelts or tiny sardines. Aim for 2–3 inches long.

People tend to be intimidated by these little fish, but have no fear, they are easy to prepare and taste simply divine. Soon, you will be using these little gems with everything. They are popular all over Spain.

To clean the anchovies, run your finger down the belly side and open up the fish. Pull the spine from the head and separate it from the flesh. Remove the head. Wash the fish and let dry on paper towels.

Put the anchovies in a plastic container and pour in the vinegar. Let marinate in the refrigerator overnight. Rinse the anchovies and put in a serving dish with the garlic, parsley, and oil, cover and chill overnight in the refrigerator. Return to room temperature before serving with bread or as an accompaniment to another dish. You can return them to the refrigerator to eat another day— they only get better with time.

PINCHOS

Pinchos are little morsels which are usually eaten on an honesty system. You help yourself to the different varieties on display. Generally, they are eaten without a plate, and in some bars you are charged according to the number of toothpicks you've used.

Put the oil, garlic, pepper flakes, and thyme in a saucepan, bring to a boil, then remove from the heat. Let cool.

Put the asparagus in a blender and pulse until smooth. Slowly add the strained oil and blend again. Mix in the ground almonds and salt and pepper to taste.

Slice the pimiento into thin strips. Spoon the asparagus mixture onto the sliced bread and top with the sliced pimiento. Add a few thyme leaves and serve on a tray for your guests to help themselves.

2 tablespoons olive oil

1 garlic clove, crushed

½ teaspoon hot red pepper flakes

leaves from
2 sprigs of thyme

4 oz. white asparagus, in can or jar*

2 tablespoons slivered almonds, ground to a paste with a mortar and pestle

½ canned pimiento, chopped

8 slices of white bread, lightly toasted

sea salt and freshly ground black pepper

SERVES 4

*White asparagus, sold in cans or jars, is a traditional Spanish ingredient.

MARINATED BLACK OLIVES

Oily black olives are the best variety for this recipe, because their soft texture and residual oil suit the spicy, sharp flavors of the marinade. Marinate for as long as possible—at least a month. They will keep for several months—just mix and taste occasionally.

Drain the olives of their brine, reserving a little for refilling. Put the olives in a bowl, add the garlic, chiles, peppercorns, lemon, parsley, bay leaves, and salt. Mix, then transfer to a jar into which they just fit, then pour over the vinegar and the reserved brine. Shake well and let marinate at room temperature for 2 weeks.

about 1 lb. black Spanish olives in brine

4 garlic cloves, sliced

2 dried red chiles

8 black peppercorns

1 slice of lemon

4 sprigs of parsley

4 fresh bay leaves

a pinch of salt

1¼ cups red wine vinegar

SERVES 4

MARINATED GREEN OLIVES

I like to use firm green olives for this recipe. The crunchy texture remains during marinating. This mix of flavors is typical of Andalusia. Most of Spain's green olives grow in this region—one whiff and you're reminded immediately of southern Spain.

Put the olives in a bowl with the garlic, coriander, fennel, thyme, rosemary, orange zest, and juice. Stir, then transfer to a glass bottle into which they just fit. Cover with olive oil, shake well, and let marinate at room temperature for at least 6 days.

about 1 lb. large green Spanish olives in brine, drained

6 garlic cloves, crushed

1 tablespoon coriander seeds, lightly crushed

1 tablespoon fennel seeds, lightly crushed

6 sprigs of thyme, bruised

4 sprigs of rosemary, bruised

grated zest and freshly squeezed juice of 1 unwaxed orange

olive oil

SERVES 4

SALTED ALMONDS

Almond trees were originally brought to Spain by the Moors and flourished especially around Seville. Salted almonds as tapas are seen more often here than any other city.

2 cups whole blanched almonds, about 8 oz.

1 teaspoon coarse salt or sea salt, finely ground

½ teaspoon oak-smoked sweet Spanish paprika (*pimentón dulce*)

olive oil, for cooking

SERVES 4

Pour 1 inch depth of oil into a saucepan and heat to 380°F. Test with a candy thermometer, or drop in a small cube of bread—it should turn golden in about 30 seconds.

Sauté the almonds until lightly golden. Drain, sprinkle with the salt and paprika, and mix well.

Let cool slightly before serving.

ALIOLI

Alioli is the garlic-laden version of the Spanish mayonnaise, mahonesa, thought to have originated in Mahon, the capital of the island of Menorca. To help stop it separating, have all the ingredients at room temperature, perhaps slightly warming the oil first—then adding in stages, not in a steady stream as some books recommend.

4–6 garlic cloves, crushed

1 whole egg

1 egg yolk

1 teaspoon freshly squeezed lemon juice

2 cups olive oil

sea salt and freshly ground black pepper

SERVES 4

Put the garlic, egg, egg yolk, and lemon juice in a food processor. Blend until pale yellow. Keeping the machine running, slowly pour in the olive oil, a bit at a time. Blend well, until thick and silky, then add salt and pepper to taste. Serve at room temperature with fish or meat.

ALIOLI WITH POTATOES

Put 1 lb. unpeeled new potatoes in a saucepan, cover with cold water, add a pinch of salt, and boil until tender. Drain and let cool. Slip off the skins, cut the potatoes into bite-size pieces, then serve with alioli as a dip.

meat and poultry

ALBÓNDIGAS
MEATBALLS IN TOMATO SAUCE

6 oz. ground pork

6 oz. ground veal

1 teaspoon freshly
squeezed lemon juice

½ small onion,
finely chopped

2 garlic cloves, crushed

2 tablespoons freshly
chopped flat-leaf
parsley

½ teaspoon freshly
grated nutmeg

½ teaspoon ground
cloves

¼ cup dried bread
crumbs

1 egg

1 tablespoon
light cream

all-purpose flour,
for dusting

2 tablespoons olive oil

sea salt and freshly
ground white pepper

TOMATO SAUCE

½ cup white wine

14 oz. canned chopped
tomatoes

½ small onion, finely
chopped

2 garlic cloves, crushed

½ teaspoon oak-smoked
sweet Spanish paprika
(*pimentón dulce*)

1 fresh bay leaf

SERVES 4

This dish was one of my first tapas experiences.
I remember the meat being so tender it just
melted in my mouth. Some serve meatballs with
alioli and lemon. They reheat well and even
taste better that way.

To make the meatballs, put the pork and veal in a bowl,
then add the lemon juice, onion, garlic, parsley,
nutmeg, cloves, breadcrumbs, egg, cream, salt, and
pepper. Mix well, then roll into walnut-size balls.
Dust with flour.

Heat the oil in a casserole dish until smoking, add
the meatballs, and sauté until browned on all sides.
Reduce the heat to low. Add the wine, tomatoes, onions,
garlic, paprika, bay leaf, and ⅓ cup water. Cover and
simmer for 1 hour. The mixture should be quite liquid,
so add extra water if necessary. Serve warm.

CHORIZO AL VINO
CHORIZO IN RED WINE

1 tablespoon olive oil

10 oz. small, spicy fresh chorizo sausages, cut into ½-inch slices

½ cup red wine

crusty bread, to serve

SERVES 4

Chorizo comes in many different varieties. You can get smoked, unsmoked, fresh, and cured. I suggest spicy fresh chorizo, available in Mexican markets. The rich color and pungent flavor come from the large quantities of paprika used to make it. Each region has its own traditional recipe—this one is simple and delicious.

Put the oil in a heavy skillet and heat until smoking. Add the chorizo and cook for 1 minute. Reduce the heat, add the wine, and cook for 5 minutes. Transfer to a serving dish and set aside to develop the flavors. Serve warm with crusty bread.

CROQUETAS DE JAMÓN
HAM AND CHICKEN CROQUETTES

Jamón serrano, Spanish mountain ham, is one of Spain's greatest culinary creations. It is pungent, sweet, and slightly salty—a key ingredient in many Spanish recipes. Mixed with creamy ingredients, it is a surprise filling for this crisp and crunchy tapas favorite.

1 cup milk

½ small onion, sliced

1 bay leaf

2 peppercorns

a sprig of thyme

2 tablespoons unsalted butter

3 tablespoons all-purpose flour

a pinch of oak-smoked sweet Spanish paprika (*pimentón dulce*)

a pinch of freshly grated nutmeg

6 oz. jamón serrano (Spanish ham), prosciutto, or Smithfield, finely chopped

4 oz. cooked chicken breast, finely chopped

2 cups dried bread crumbs

2 eggs, lightly beaten

oil, for cooking and deep-frying

an electric deep-fryer

SERVES 4

Put the milk in a saucepan, add the onion, bay leaf, peppercorns, and thyme and heat until just below boiling point. Remove from the heat, let cool, then strain into a bowl.

Put the butter in the saucepan, melt gently, stir in the flour, and cook for 2 minutes, stirring constantly. When the roux begins to brown, slowly add the strained milk, stirring to prevent lumps forming. Continue to cook, stirring in the paprika and nutmeg.

Heat 1 tablespoon oil in a small skillet, add the jamón, and sauté until the fat starts to fun. Add the ham and chicken to the white sauce and continue cooking until the sauce thickens, about 2 minutes.

Remove from the heat and let cool. Refrigerate for 3 hours or overnight. Shape the mixture into croquettes about 1 x 2 inches. Lightly roll in the bread crumbs, dip in the eggs, and roll in the bread crumbs again. Chill for 1 hour or overnight.

When ready to cook, fill a saucepan or deep-fryer one-third full of oil or to the manufacturer's recommended level and heat to 380°F. Add the croquettes and fry, in batches if necessary, for 3 minutes or until golden brown. Serve immediately.

CORDERO AL LIMÓN
LAMB WITH LEMON

8 oz. lean lamb

8 oz. canned
pineapple slices

10 cloves

1 lemon, halved

5 garlic cloves

2 tablespoons olive oil

a sprig of rosemary

½ small onion,
finely chopped

a pinch of oak-smoked
sweet Spanish paprika
(*pimentón dulce*)

SERVES 4

This recipe is a favorite in Aragón and Murcia in central Spain, where meat-based tapas are popular. The use of pineapple for tenderizing meat is a technique found in Southeast Asia. Perhaps it arrived in Spain from the former Spanish colony of the Philippines. Serve this tapas with a good Rioja.

Cut the lamb into ¾-inch cubes, put in a bowl, cover with the pineapple slices, cover, and let marinate overnight in the refrigerator.

Push the cloves into the lemon and put it in a roasting dish. Add the garlic, oil, and rosemary. Remove the lamb from the pineapple and rub in the onion and paprika. Add the lamb to the roasting dish and cook in a preheated oven at 300°F for 15 minutes. Remove the dish from the oven, cover with foil, and set aside for 10 minutes before serving.

PINCHITOS MORUNOS
SPICY MOORISH KABOBS

This recipe is from Andalusia, where you see it in almost every tapas bar. The area is renowned for simple food, so this is a quick, easy recipe which leaves more time for other things, like chatting with friends.

2 tablespoons olive oil

2 garlic cloves, crushed

1 dried red chile, crushed

1 teaspoon ground cumin

1 teaspoon ground fennel

1 teaspoon oak-smoked sweet Spanish paprika (*pimentón dulce*)

freshly squeezed juice of 1 lemon

2 tablespoons freshly chopped flat-leaf parsley

1 tablespoon dry sherry

1 lb. pork tenderloin

metal kabob skewers, or bamboo, soaked in water for 30 minutes

SERVES 4

Put the oil, garlic, chile, cumin, fennel, paprika, lemon juice, parsley, and sherry in a bowl and mix well. Cut the pork into ¾-inch cubes and add to the bowl. Cover and chill overnight in the refrigerator.

When ready to cook, preheat a broiler until very hot. Thread the pork onto the skewers and broil for 10 minutes, turning often—take care not to overcook the meat. Remove from the heat and set aside for 10 minutes. Serve warm.

8 chicken wings

1 teaspoon oak-smoked sweet Spanish paprika (*pimentón dulce*)

1 tablespoon freshly squeezed lemon juice

2 tablespoons oil

6 garlic cloves, coarsely crushed

⅔ cup brandy, preferably Spanish

sea salt and freshly ground black pepper

SERVES 4

POLLO AL AJILLO
CHICKEN WITH GARLIC

This dish finds it way onto almost every tapas menu in Spain and varies only slightly. It's very common, yet so simple.

Put the chicken wings in a bowl, then rub the paprika evenly over the skin. Add the lemon juice, cover, and let marinate in the refrigerator for 2 hours.

Heat the oil in a heavy skillet until smoking, add the chicken, and brown on all sides. Reduce the heat, add the garlic, and cook for a further 2 minutes. Add the brandy, tilt the pan to catch the flame, and burn off the alcohol until the flames subside. Cover the pan with a lid and simmer for 10 minutes. Add salt and pepper to taste, then serve.

EMPANADILLAS DE CARNE
PORK AND VEAL TURNOVERS

These small, savory pies are great to serve with other tapas. They can be made days in advance and can even be frozen.

To make the dough, put the lemon juice, butter, and a scant ½ cup water in a saucepan, heat until melted, and then let cool. When cool, sift in the flour and salt and mix slowly. Knead on a floured surface until the mixture loses its stickiness. Wrap in plastic wrap and refrigerate for 2 hours.

Meanwhile, to make the stuffing, heat the oil in a skillet. Add the onion, garlic, pork, and veal, cook for 3 minutes, add the tomato paste, wine, oregano, and parsley, then cook for 5 minutes. Remove from the heat, season well, and add the hard-cooked egg. Chill.

Put the dough on a floured surface and roll out to ⅛-inch thickness. Cut into 3-inch rounds and spoon a heaping teaspoon into the center of the circle. Brush the edges with water and fold in half. Using your index fingers, push the edges together to create a ribbon effect.

Fill a deep-fryer with oil to the manufacturer's recommended level and heat to 380°F. Working in batches, dip each turnover in the beaten egg mixture, deep-fry for 3 minutes until golden brown, then serve.

freshly squeezed juice of 1 lemon

1 stick butter

1½ cups all-purpose flour

a pinch of sea salt

STUFFING

1 tablespoon olive oil

1 tablespoon finely grated onion

1 garlic clove, crushed

4 oz. ground pork

4 oz. ground veal

1 tablespoon tomato paste

1 tablespoon white wine

1 teaspoon dried oregano

1 teaspoon chopped fresh parsley

1 hard-cooked egg, mashed

2 eggs lightly beaten with
2 tablespoons water

sea salt and freshly ground
white pepper

oil, for frying

a cookie cutter, 3 inches diameter

an electric deep-fryer

SERVES 4

fish and seafood

ALMEJAS A LA MARINERA
CLAMS IN TOMATO AND SAFFRON SAUCE

Spain has the longest coastline in Europe. Therefore, seafood forms a major part of the Spanish diet. Almejas (clams) are popular, especially in Catalonia. They are easy to cook and always delicious. You can simply steam them in white wine or sherry. However, the sweetness of the tomatoes and saffron is especially delicious.

1 lb. small fresh clams, in the shell

a pinch of saffron threads

1 tablespoon olive oil

½ small onion, finely chopped

2 garlic cloves, crushed

⅓ cup dry sherry

2 tablespoons tomato paste

1 tablespoon freshly chopped flat-leaf parsley

a pinch of oak-smoked sweet Spanish paprika (*pimentón dulce*)

a pinch of cayenne

2 tablespoons slivered almonds

SERVES 4

To clean the clams, put them in a bowl of cold salty water and let soak for 2 hours. This should help get rid of some of the grit. Put the saffron in a bowl with 1 tablespoon hot water and let soak.

Heat the oil in a casserole dish over gentle heat, then add the onion and cook for 3 minutes. Add the garlic, sherry, tomato paste, parsley, paprika, cayenne, saffron with its juice, and ¼ cup water. Bring to a boil and boil for 4 minutes.

Meanwhile, grind the almonds to a powder using a mortar and pestle.

Add the clams, cover with a lid, and cook for 4 minutes until the shells steam open (discard any that don't). Stir in the ground almonds and cook for 1 further minute. Remove the casserole dish from the heat and set aside, covered with a lid, for 5 minutes. Serve warm with bread.

CALAMARES A LA ROMANA
FRIED SQUID ROMAN-STYLE

This classic tapas dish is served just about everywhere in Spain. The best one I've tried was in a little tasca in San Sebastian. After a day on the beach, there is nothing better than a glass of cold wine with calamares. The way to make them tender is to buy small squid and not cook them too long.

1 lb. small squid, or 6 oz. cleaned squid tubes

2 eggs

all-purpose flour, for dusting

sea salt

olive oil, for frying

1 lemon, cut into wedges

an electric deep-fryer

SERVES 4

To clean the squid, pull the head away from the body (tube). Rub your thumb down the length of the tube and lever off the wings and discard. Remove the translucent quill inside and rub the pink skin off the outside. Wash well under cold water. Cut the tubes into ½-inch slices.

Put the eggs in a bowl, add 2 tablespoons water, and beat well. Put the flour on a plate and sprinkle generously with salt. Working on one at a time, dip the squid rings into the egg mixture, then into the flour, making sure they are well coated. Set aside.

Fill a deep-fryer with oil to the manufacturer's recommended level and heat to 380°F. Working in batches, cook the squid rings until golden brown. (Make sure that the temperature remains the same for each batch.) Remove with a slotted spoon and drain on crumpled paper towels. Let rest for 5 minutes, then serve with the lemon wedges.

MEJILLONES RELLENOS
STUFFED MUSSELS

12–16 fresh mussels,
in the shell

½ cup white wine

2 garlic cloves

1 teaspoon olive oil

1 small onion,
finely grated

1 tablespoon finely
chopped jamón serrano
(Spanish ham),
prosciutto, or Smithfield

1 teaspoon tomato paste

1 teaspoon finely
chopped fresh flat-leaf
parsley

oil, for deep-frying

WHITE SAUCE

2 tablespoons butter

⅓ cup all-purpose flour

scant ½ cup milk

1 egg, beaten with
1 tablespoon water

⅔ cup dried white
breadcrumbs

sea salt and freshly
ground white pepper

an electric deep-fryer

SERVES 4

A popular dish on the Madrid tapas bar circuit. Once you've tried this little number I promise you'll be back for more. A great entertaining choice, because you can prepare it in advance and it's quick to cook.

To clean the mussels, scrub them in cold water and pull off the beards. Tap them against a work surface and discard any that don't close.

Put them in a saucepan with the wine and garlic, cover, and heat until they open. Remove as soon as they do, and discard any that don't. Remove the mussels from the shells and chop the flesh. Strain the cooking liquid through a fine strainer and reserve it.

Heat the oil in a skillet, then add the onion and jamón. Cook for 3 minutes over low heat, then add the tomato paste, parsley, chopped mussels, and 2 tablespoons of the reserved mussel liquid. Stir well and cook for 1 minute. Remove from the heat and let cool.

To make the white sauce, melt the butter in a saucepan, add the flour, and cook, stirring, for 1 minute to burst the starch grains. Slowly pour in the milk, stirring all the time. Cook over low heat until the sauce is thick. Add salt and pepper to taste and let cool. Clean half the mussel shells and discard the remainder. Put 1 teaspoon of the mussel mixture in each half shell, smoothing the top with the back of a spoon. Put a teaspoon of white sauce on top of each one, then arrange on a plate, cover, and chill overnight.

Put the beaten egg in a bowl. Put the bread crumbs on a plate. Dip the mussels in the egg, then roll in the bread crumbs. Fill a deep-fryer with oil to the manufacturer's recommended level and heat to 380°F. Add the mussels in batches and fry until golden brown. Remove with a slotted spoon and drain on crumpled paper towels. Serve hot.

SARDINAS EN ESCABECHE
MARINATED SARDINES

8 fresh sardines, about 1 lb.

2 tablespoons olive oil

scant ½ cup good-quality white wine vinegar

scant ½ cup dry white wine

2 garlic cloves, sliced

4 fresh bay leaves

1 teaspoon fennel seeds, lightly crushed

½ teaspoon hot red pepper flakes

2 sprigs of thyme

4 slices of lemon

crusty bread, to serve

SERVES 4

Escabeche, which means 'pickle', is a very old method for preserving food, especially fish. The pickle effectively 'cooks' the flesh in lemon juice or vinegar. This one is in vinegar, which is perfect with the healthy, sweet oiliness of sardines. Don't be put off by cleaning the fish—it's easy, and as soon as you get the hang of these little ones you'll be cleaning bigger fish in no time.

To clean the sardines, wash them in cold water and scrape off any scales. Put the fish on a board, take off the head, run a knife from the head halfway down the belly side and scrape out the insides. Wash the fish and leave on a dish towel to dry. Run your thumb down the inside of the fish along the bone and squash the fillets flat. Gently pull the backbone away from the flesh towards the tail. Cut with scissors.

Heat the olive oil in a heavy skillet, add the vinegar, white wine, garlic, bay leaves, fennel, pepper flakes, and thyme, then bring to a boil for 3 minutes. Add the sardines skin side up, then remove from the heat.

Arrange the sardines in a single layer in a plastic or ceramic dish, put the slices of lemon on top, then pour over the liquid and cover with plastic wrap. Let marinate in the refrigerator overnight. Serve at room temperature with crusty bread.

PULPO A LA VINAGRETA
MARINATED OCTOPUS

about 12 oz. small octopus tentacles

3 tablespoons fruity olive oil

2 tablespoons red wine vinegar

2 garlic cloves, crushed

3 tablespoons freshly chopped flat-leaf parsley

½ teaspoon oak-smoked sweet Spanish paprika (*pimentón dulce*)

½ teaspoon hot red pepper flakes

1 tablespoon capers, chopped

freshly squeezed juice of 1 lemon

sea salt and freshly ground black pepper

SERVES 4

Some people avoid cooking octopus because they think it can be tough. In Spain, fresh octopus are banged against the jetty by the fishermen to make them tender. If you don't have a fisherman on hand, buy octopus frozen (freezing also helps tenderize them). Then you should cook them long and slow at a low temperature. Octopus keeps well, and the longer you marinate it, the better the flavor.

Bring a large saucepan of water to a boil, then blanch the octopus for 30 seconds at a time, repeating 4–5 times. Return the octopus to the saucepan, cover with a lid, and simmer for 1 hour.

Test the octopus for tenderness—if it's still tough, continue cooking for another 20 minutes. Remove from the heat, let cool, then drain. Cut the tentacles into 1-inch lengths.

Heat the oil in a skillet, add the vinegar, garlic, 2 tablespoons of the parsley, paprika, pepper flakes, capers, and octopus. Bring to a boil, then simmer for 3 minutes. Transfer to a plastic or ceramic dish, let cool, season, then let marinate in the refrigerator overnight.

Serve at room temperature with lemon juice and the remaining parsley.

GAMBAS A LA GABARDINA
SHRIMP IN OVERCOATS

10 oz. uncooked shrimp, shell on

¾ cup all-purpose flour

1 teaspoon baking powder

a pinch of salt

a pinch of oak-smoked sweet Spanish paprika (*pimentón dulce*)

1 cup beer

oil, for frying

lemon wedges, to serve

an electric deep-fryer

SERVES 4

I first tasted this dish in a tapas bar in Barcelona and it was just perfect with a cold beer. It is a simple recipe and can be whipped up in no time at all. This method of deep-frying will make the batter crisp, while the shrimp remain tender and juicy inside. Cook them in small batches so as not to reduce the temperature of the oil.

Peel the shrimp, but leave the tail fins intact. Sift the flour, baking powder, salt, and paprika into a bowl, mix well, then pour in the beer. Let rest for a few minutes.

Fill a deep-fryer with oil to the manufacturer's recommended level and heat the oil to 380°F. Dip the shrimp in the batter, cook in the oil until golden brown, drain on paper towels, and serve with lemon wedges.

ALBÓNDIGAS DE BACALAO
COD BALLS

4 oz. salt cod

10 oz. potatoes

1 bay leaf

1 garlic clove, crushed

1 tablespoon freshly chopped flat-leaf parsley

freshly ground white pepper

1 egg

all-purpose flour

oil, for frying

lemon wedges

alioli (page 20)

an electric deep-fryer

SERVES 4

Dried salt cod is known as bacalao in Spain. It can be found in Spanish delis as well as Caribbean and Italian stores. Though Spain is seafood-mad, with fresh fish of all kinds widely available, salt cod has an almost religious significance. In fact, that is the origin of its popularity in Catholic southern Europe—as a reliable source of fish for the Friday fast. It must be soaked to soften it and to remove the majority of the salt. If you find it hard to buy, substitute another meaty white fish and halve the cooking time.

Put the cod in a bowl, cover with cold water, and keep in the refrigerator for at least 24 hours, changing the water occasionally.

Prick the potatoes with a skewer, then roast in a preheated oven at 400°F for 1 hour or until soft on the inside. Remove from the oven, scoop the flesh out of the skins into a bowl, and mash.

Put the cod in a saucepan, cover with cold water, add the bay leaf, bring to a boil, and simmer for 30 minutes. Remove from the heat and let cool. Remove the skin and flake the flesh into a bowl, making sure to remove all the bones. Add the flesh to the mashed potatoes, then stir in the garlic, parsley, pepper, and

2 tablespoons of the cod cooking liquid. Roll the mixture into balls about the size of a walnut. Put in a bowl, cover with plastic wrap, and chill in the refrigerator for 2–3 hours until firm.

Put the egg in a bowl, add 1 tablespoon water, and beat lightly. Put the flour on a plate. Dip the cod balls in the egg, then roll in the flour.

Fill a deep-fryer with oil to the manufacturer's recommended level and heat to 380°F. Cook the balls, in batches if necessary, for about 3 minutes or until golden brown. Remove with a slotted spoon and drain on crumpled paper towels.

Serve hot with alioli and lemon wedges.

PIMIENTOS RELLENOS DE BACALAO
PEPPERS STUFFED WITH SALT COD

Salt cod is typically Spanish (see page 46 for suggestions on where to buy it). If difficult to find, substitute any other white fish, omit the soaking time, and simmer for just 5 minutes. Piquillo peppers are grown in the Navarra region in the north of Spain. They are slightly sour and very small, so perfect for tapas.

6 oz. salt cod

scant 1 cup milk

1 small onion, finely sliced

2 bay leaves

a sprig of parsley

2 tablespoons unsalted butter

2 tablespoons all-purpose flour

8 canned piquillo peppers, drained

sea salt and freshly ground white pepper

sliced bread, to serve (optional)

SERVES 4

Put the cod in a bowl, cover with cold water, and keep in the refrigerator for at least 24 hours, changing the water occasionally.

Put the milk in a saucepan, then add the onion, bay leaf, and parsley. Heat almost to boiling, then remove from the heat and let cool.

Melt the butter in a saucepan, then stir in the flour and cook for 1 minute. Slowly stir in the strained milk. Cook over medium heat for 3 minutes or until the mixture is thick. Season with salt and pepper and let cool.

Drain the cod, put in a saucepan, cover with cold water, bring to a boil, then simmer for 20 minutes. Remove and pat dry with paper towels. Remove the skin and flake the flesh into a bowl, making sure to remove all the bones. Pour in the white sauce and mix well. Stuff into the cavity of the peppers. Chill for 2 hours or overnight. Bake in a preheated oven at 300°F for 15 minutes. Serve in a bowl or on sliced bread.

vegetables

CHAMPIÑONES AL AILLO
MUSHROOMS IN GARLIC SAUCE

This dish is great for any season, because you can get mushrooms all year round. I suggest using regular mushrooms, but you can use other varieties. I, like the Spaniards, love garlic and in an ideal world would put it on everything. Feel free to add more: cook as you please.

Cut the larger mushrooms in half and set aside. Heat the oil in a heavy skillet and add all the mushrooms, garlic, and chile. Toss to coat with the oil, then cook for 2 minutes. Add the sherry, broth, and paprika, cook for a further 2 minutes, then add salt and pepper to taste. Serve warm.

4 oz. small to medium mushrooms

1 tablespoon olive oil

4 garlic cloves, thinly sliced

½ fresh mild red chile, seeded and finely sliced

¼ cup dry sherry

3 tablespoons chicken broth

a pinch of oak-smoked sweet Spanish paprika (*pimentón dulce*)

sea salt and freshly ground white pepper

SERVES 4

PIMIENTOS PICANTES
MARINATED BELL PEPPERS

Marinated bell peppers are very simple, but taste fantastic; for best results, use small ones. Serve on a slice of bread or toast, or go that bit further and serve the bread old-fashioned tapas-style, on top of a glass of chilled sherry.

3 small red bell peppers

3 tablespoons olive oil

¼ cup sherry vinegar

a sprig of thyme

a sprig of rosemary

2 garlic cloves, sliced

½ teaspoon cayenne

1 tablespoon salted capers, rinsed and drained

1 tablespoon freshly chopped flat-leaf parsley

sea salt and freshly ground white pepper

thinly sliced bread, to serve

SERVES 4

Broil the whole peppers slowly until the skins are blistered and black. Transfer to a plastic bag, seal, and let steam. When cool, pull off the skins and remove the seeds and membranes. Put the peppers in a strainer set over a bowl to catch the juices and cut into ½-inch strips.

Heat a heavy skillet, then add the oil, sherry, thyme, rosemary, garlic, cayenne, and the collected pepper juices. Cook over low heat for 2 minutes. Add the peppers, capers, parsley, and salt and pepper to taste. Cook, stirring, for 1 minute. Remove from the heat and let cool. Cover and chill overnight.

To serve, return to room temperature and serve on a thin slice of bread (tapas) with sherry, wine, or beer. This dish can be kept in the refrigerator for up to a week.

COLIFLOR EN ADOBO
MARINATED CAULIFLOWER

This simple dish is a great accompaniment to any other tapas. It is one I make often and keep in the refrigerator. Make sure you don't over-blanch the cauliflower—it's better when it's still crunchy.

Put the saffron threads in a bowl with 2 tablespoons hot water. Break the cauliflower into florets and slice thinly through the head and stem. Blanch in a saucepan of boiling water for 30 seconds, strain, and transfer to a bowl.

Heat the oil in a skillet, then add the whole garlic cloves, paprika, vinegar, sugar, rosemary, lemon, salt, and pepper. Let boil for 3 minutes. Add the saffron and its soaking water, then pour the mixture over the cauliflower and stir well. Cover with plastic wrap and let marinate in the refrigerator for 3 days.

Serve at room temperature, sprinkled with chopped parsley.

a pinch of saffron threads

8 oz. cauliflower

¼ cup olive oil

3 garlic cloves

½ teaspoon oak-smoked sweet Spanish paprika (*pimentón dulce*)

3 tablespoons sherry vinegar

a pinch of sugar

a sprig of rosemary

2 slices of lemon

sea salt and freshly ground white pepper

a handful of freshly chopped flat-leaf parsley, to serve

SERVES 4

3 tablespoons olive oil

1¼ lb. potatoes, cut into ¾-inch cubes

1 small onion, grated

3 garlic cloves, crushed

2 tablespoons fino sherry

4 oz. canned chopped tomatoes

½ teaspoon hot red pepper flakes, well crushed

½ teaspoon freshly grated orange zest

1 teaspoon sugar

1 tablespoon freshly chopped flat-leaf parsley

1 fresh bay leaf

SERVES 4

PATATAS BRAVAS
POTATOES IN TOMATO SAUCE

A very popular tapas dish, simple to prepare and always a good accompaniment to more complicated dishes. The orange peel is a hidden flavor which works well with the tomatoes and chile. I use it in most of my tomato sauces.

Heat 2 tablespoons of the oil in a skillet, add the potatoes, and mix well. Cook for 15 minutes until golden brown.

Meanwhile, heat the remaining oil in another skillet, add the onion, and cook gently for 5 minutes. Add the garlic and sherry, then simmer for 1 minute to burn off the alcohol. Reduce the heat and add the tomatoes, chile, orange zest, sugar, parsley, and bay leaf. Cook for 10 minutes— add water to stop the mixture thickening too much.

Transfer the cooked potatoes to a serving bowl, pour over the tomato sauce, and mix well. This can be made a day in advance and reheated before serving.

DELICIAS DE QUESO
CHEESE BALLS

Manchego cheese is popular all over Spain. It is to the Spanish what Parmesan is to the Italians. The mix of Manchego sheep cheese and Spanish goat cheese balance each other perfectly. A treat for your guests.

Put the flour and milk in a bowl and stir until smooth. Add the paprika, salt, pepper, and the whole egg. Add the garlic and both cheeses and mix well.

Put the egg whites in a bowl and whisk till stiff. Fold one-third into the flour mixture and mix well, then fold in the remaining egg whites making sure not to lose all the air. Sprinkle with the thyme and jamón.

Fill a deep-fryer with oil to the manufacturer's recommended level and heat the oil to 380°F. Using a teaspoon, run the spoon through the mixture collecting an even amount of thyme and jamón and drop a heaped spoonful into the hot oil. Cook for 3 minutes or until the mixture is golden brown. Drain on paper towels and serve immediately with toothpicks.

2 tablespoons
all-purpose flour

2 tablespoons milk

½ teaspoon oak-smoked sweet Spanish paprika (*pimentón dulce*)

1 egg

1 garlic clove, crushed

6 oz. Manchego cheese, finely grated

6 oz. goat cheese

2 egg whites

1 teaspoon chopped fresh thyme leaves

1 tablespoon finely chopped jamón serrano (Spanish ham), prosciutto, or Smithfield or ham

sea salt and freshly ground white pepper

oil, for frying

an electric deep-fryer

SERVES 4

PISTO MANCHEGO

ZUCCHINI, TOMATO, AND PEPPER STEW

This is a popular vegetable dish from central Spain. There are two types, one with meat and one without. I have used jamón in this version, but feel free not to.

Heat the oil in a skillet, add the jamón and onion, and cook over low heat for 5 minutes. Add the garlic, zucchini, tomatoes, red bell pepper, oregano, and paprika. Simmer over low heat for 15 minutes, then add salt and pepper to taste, and serve.

This recipe can be made a day in advance and reheats well.

2 tablespoons olive oil

2 oz. jamón serrano (Spanish ham), prosciutto, or Smithfield, finely chopped

½ onion, finely chopped

4 garlic cloves, crushed

1 zucchini, chopped

2 tomatoes, peeled, seeded, and chopped

½ red bell pepper, seeded and chopped

1 tablespoon chopped fresh oregano leaves

a pinch of oak-smoked sweet Spanish paprika (*pimentón dulce*)

sea salt and freshly ground white pepper

SERVES 4

CORAZONES DE ALCACHOFA MACERADOS CON AJO
ARTICHOKE HEARTS MARINATED IN GARLIC

Artichokes are easier to cook than you might think. Just make sure you remove as much of the green leaves as possible, because they can be tough. As you prepare them, put them in a bowl of cold water with a squeeze of lemon juice to stop them discoloring, and don't be afraid of overcooking them.

8 small artichokes

freshly squeezed juice of 1 lemon and grated zest of ½ unwaxed lemon

a pinch of sea salt

3 tablespoons olive oil

6 garlic cloves

a sprig of thyme

2 tablespoons Spanish red wine vinegar

a sprig of flat-leaf parsley

sea salt and freshly ground white pepper

SERVES 4

Cut off the artichoke stalks ½ inch from the base. Trim off the outer leaves and, using a potato peeler, peel the outer sections and remove the green leaves. Cut off the tip and spoon out any furry bits from the middle section (this is called the choke). As you prepare them, put them in a bowl of cold water with the lemon juice.

Bring a saucepan of salted water to a boil, add the artichoke hearts, and cook until tender, about 20 minutes. Meanwhile put the oil, garlic, thyme, and lemon zest in a small saucepan and heat gently. Remove from the heat and leave to infuse. Drain the artichokes, cut in half, and dry on paper towels. Transfer to a bowl, then add the infused oil, the vinegar, and parsley and stir well. Sprinkle with salt and pepper and let marinate in the refrigerator for 2–3 days. Serve at room temperature.

ESPINACAS CON PIÑONES Y PASAS
SPINACH, PINE NUTS, AND RAISINS

½ cup raisins

2 tablespoons fruity olive oil

½ cup pine nuts, toasted in a dry skillet

2 garlic cloves, sliced

3 tablespoons dry sherry

8 oz. fresh spinach, about 2 cups

a pinch of oak-smoked sweet Spanish paprika (*pimentón dulce*)

sea salt and freshly ground black pepper

SERVES 4

Finally a green vegetable has made its way into my tapas selection. This recipe is quick and easy, so make it right at the last minute.

Soak the raisins in warm water for 3 minutes. Drain.

Heat the oil in a skillet, add the pine nuts and garlic, cook for 1 minute, then add the sherry and boil for 1 minute.

Add the spinach and paprika and toss well to coat with the juices. Cook over low heat for 5 minutes. Add the drained raisins with salt and pepper to taste, then serve.

INDEX

conversion charts

Weights and measures have been rounded up or down slightly to make measuring easier.

Volume equivalents:

American	Metric	Imperial
1 teaspoon	5 ml	
1 tablespoon	15 ml	
¼ cup	60 ml	2 fl.oz.
⅓ cup	75 ml	2½ fl.oz.
½ cup	125 ml	4 fl.oz.
⅔ cup	150 ml	5 fl.oz. (¼ pint)
¾ cup	175 ml	6 fl.oz.
1 cup	250 ml	8 fl.oz.

Weight equivalents:

Imperial	Metric
1 oz.	25 g
2 oz.	50 g
3 oz.	75 g
4 oz.	125 g
5 oz.	150 g
6 oz.	175 g
7 oz.	200 g
8 oz. (½ lb.)	250 g
9 oz.	275 g
10 oz.	300 g
11 oz.	325 g
12 oz.	375 g
13 oz.	400 g
14 oz.	425 g
15 oz.	475 g
16 oz. (1 lb.)	500 g
2 lb.	1 kg

Measurements:

Inches	Cm
¼ inch	5 mm
½ inch	1 cm
¾ inch	1.5 cm
1 inch	2.5 cm
2 inches	5 cm
3 inches	7 cm
4 inches	10 cm
5 inches	12 cm
6 inches	15 cm
7 inches	18 cm
8 inches	20 cm
9 inches	23 cm
10 inches	25 cm
11 inches	28 cm
12 inches	30 cm

Oven temperatures:

110°C	(225°F)	Gas ¼
120°C	(250°F)	Gas ½
140°C	(275°F)	Gas 1
150°C	(300°F)	Gas 2
160°C	(325°F)	Gas 3
180°C	(350°F)	Gas 4
190°C	(375°F)	Gas 5
200°C	(400°F)	Gas 6
220°C	(425°F)	Gas 7
230°C	(450°F)	Gas 8
240°C	(475°F)	Gas 9